IT'S JUST A PHASE

IT'S JUST A PHASE

RAY ZIMMERMAN

WALNUT STREET
PUBLISHING

Cover Photo: Luna Moth by Ray Zimmerman
ISBN 979-8-9909790-2-4

Walnut Street Publishing
1673 S Holtzclaw Ave
Chattanooga, TN 37404

Introduction

Many of these pieces are inspired by the Natural World, but some are drawn from other experiences. Some are quite serious, but they all flowed quickly from my pen. I hope you have as much fun reading them as I did while writing them.

The photographs and drawings are my own. For years, I was told that I could not draw. At age 71, I attended a nature journaling workshop which I expected to be a writing experience. I nearly bolted from the room when I learned it was drawing, but I am glad I stayed. A very patient teacher helped me bring forth some drawings. Now, my creative works include drawing.

Thanks, and Happy Reading.
Ray Zimmerman

The Poems in Order of Appearance

To a Luna Moth

How strange you appear to my eye,
with powdered wings to bear you aloft
to heights that I will never reach.

Mouthless you left eating behind
with that caterpillar skin you shed.
Do you feel the pangs of hunger?

Those feather antennae direct your life.
They detect the scent of a female
a mile or more away, and off you go.

You live a few brief days
to leave your legacy of caterpillars.
So alien, so beautiful, so human.

Villanelle for the Didgeridoo

We all should try the didgeridoo.
With practice, I'm sure I could learn how to play.
It would make me happy. How about you?

With that honking noise, the birds all flew.
The upstairs neighbors have moved away.
We all should try the didgeridoo.

Uninvited guests are suddenly few.
Those who arrived have promised to pray.
It would make me happy. How about you?

My new friends now say they love it for true.
They sit and listen with never a fray.
We all should try the didgeridoo.

With time, my musical repertoire grew.
I charmed a small dog, the neighborhood stray.
It would make me happy. How about you?

Broken, I quickly repaired it with glue.
I'd love to say more, but I cannot stay.
We all should try the didgeridoo.
It would make me happy. How about you?

A Chattanooga Lookout

The Lookouts got their first shot at fame,
a New York Yankees Exhibition game.

They signed Jackie Mitchell, a publicity stunt,
but she pitched like a pro, not some sorry runt.

The starter gave up a hit and a double.
They sent Jackie in to heal this trouble.

She struck out Babe Ruth, third up to bat.
She struck out Lou Gehrig, imagine that.

Lazzeri, she walked, put a third man on base.
The manager pulled her just to save face.

The commissioner said that she had to go.
Should women play baseball? He just said no.

But Jackie achieved House of David fame.
That barnstorming team won many-a-game.

The men all wore beards and long hair to boot.
She wore a fake beard and thought it was a hoot.

At age 17 she established her name and now
is remembered in the Baseball Hall of Fame.

Late August Collage

Begin with the yellow flowers of a Jerusalem artichoke. Make strands of its essence. They are warp and woof, a framework for your tapestry.

Weave in the golden brown of coreopsis and the pink of cone-flower. Add the red from a fireweed, and you have made a start.

Weave in the rich brown feather of a wren dropped near her empty nest.

Eggshells make a nice touch if you can find them.

Hang your tapestry from a hickory branch. Let it ripen with the nuts.

When the time is right, add lichen: the kind known as "old man's beard," the ephemeral green vessels called "pixie cups," and the red-topped "British soldiers."

Let it bake in the August sun and steep in the lightning of sudden storms.

It will hide its eyes from the pounding rain and soften in the nur-turing mists.

Now your tapestry is ready to receive the gentle songs of chicka-dees and nuthatches.

Let the pileated woodpecker drop chips from his drill as he feeds on carpenter ants. A few will stick.

Seek the help of a spider. Her silk will bind the work together.

4

Hang your tapestry on your wall if you must. Spiderlings will hatch from its threads. You will know it belongs in the woods.

This change will happen at the time of day when the buzzing of cicadas gives way to the trills of katydids.

Hang it on your porch. Let the light from Altair and Deneb illuminate its recesses.

It will waffle in the breeze of early morning as bats retire to take their daytime rest.

Ask yourself, "Have I woven this tapestry, or has it woven me?"

Driving to New Hope

I sense the day is wasted
when I haven't seen the dawn.
One morning I left early,
and drove the mountain road,
with a blue-black sky above,
as trees blocked light from left and right.
With sky and sun hidden from view
I thought of sunrise and beginnings.
I turned the curve before
descending to the valley below.
I greeted a sky as red as
the belly of a rainbow trout,
edged by the dark of Missionary Ridge.
The red sky above gave way to blue.

Prom Night

Amorous alligators awaken to red-rimmed skies.
Sun going down, they bellow bellicose greetings
across the swamp.

Looking for some action,
a dominant male slaps silent water with his jaw.

Lesser males leave the pond
to seek action elsewhere.
They wander through subdivisions.

Amorous alligators arrive on decks and porches,
to bask beneath lawn sprinklers.

They give a new meaning to an old country song,
"Looking for Love in All the Wrong Places."

One should not fool with
amorous alligators high on hormones.

Watchful wildlife officers arrive to relocate them.
They restrict the movements of amorous alligators.

The Names of Trees

Smoke curled skyward as trees forgot their names,
oak leaf and maple leaf first desiccated,
robbed of moisture, and then incinerated
in a no-disco inferno, they curled and fell.

They forgot their names, just as my father
on his invalid bed forgot my name and then
his own before the coma took him
to fly like an eagle as promised by Isaiah.

This morning the sun burned through
the cellophane red maple leaves behind the house.
Thin as my elderly father's skin they gave the light
an appearance of Christmastide.

Fly Fishing

When I was young and sad
I carried a rod of the finest cane
to a Kansas farm pond.
I popped the blue gill with
a deer hair popper.

At the next pond up
I tried a Domino Nymph.
Black and white it shone.
I don't know what insect
it was meant to imitate.

You dove deep with that fly,
as I kept the rod tip high.
You tail-walked across the pond,
broke the line and were gone,
bigger than any bass I had ever caught.

From that day since
Nature has been my solace,
perhaps from even before,
but you cemented my naturalist persona
and I knew I would always be a fisherman.

Speaking of Nature

I Kali

Shall I speak to you of nature?
I shall, but I must give a warning.
Kali, the patron goddess of Kolkata,
is a nature goddess. She personifies
the destructive forces of nature.

Kali rules typhoons and earthquakes.
The tidal wave is in her domain.
She wears a necklace of human skulls.
She is the bringer of enlightenment,
but her wisdom has a price.

Aerial photographs of an area hit by a typhoon.
reveal human bodies awash in an ocean.
Some may be alive and waving hands
in hopes of summoning an unlikely rescue.

We moderns want new beginnings,
without endings, gain without sacrifice.
and unity without reconciliation.
Kali puts an end to such foolishness.

She is an incarnation of Shiva's wife.
She is sometimes depicted with
her foot on her husband's chest,
his heart in her upraised hand.

II Fecundity

You say, "Speak to us of Nature,"
and I reply, Nature is a messy business.
Be forewarned: life begets life.

Ancient peoples saw the planet Venus
appearing for nine months at a time
and she became a fertility goddess.

She governed erotic love.
Her appearance stimulated human impulses,
and the mating of livestock and wildlife.

Gray whales on their way to Baja are bound
for an ancient ritual. Every gray whale calf
was conceived in those mystic waters.

The mother whales will travel to
Arctic feeding grounds and back
To deliver one-ton infants.

Twelve months in the making,
they stick close to Mom for a trip
to the arctic and back.

III Buffalo Bull

Where have my prairies gone,
with the big bluestem and
compass plant that tickled my belly?

They have been plowed and
planted with corn and wheat
as the plowman's children sang.
Oh, give me a home
where the buffalo roam.

We fed the native people
for centuries and they honored
us in their ceremonies.
A buffalo skull was a sacred object.
We had an agreement with them.

We took care of the land.
The prairie grass thrived
as we trampled tree seedlings
and devoured them. We had
an agreement with the grass.

The cowbirds followed us and
ate the insects we stirred up.
Today, they follow the brown and
white cattle that belong to
ranchers who need no agreement.

I will not apologize to the family
of the photographer that my brother
killed after being kicked.
That man got what he wanted,
a buffalo in a different pose.

IV Wolf

Shall I speak to you of nature?
Are you certain?
I shall tell you that predators are essential.

When wolves returned to Yellowstone
they happily set about killing elk.

Trees browsed to anemic decline recovered,
and the forest regained its health. The herds
became strong under the predators' watchful eye.

Beavers returned and dammed the streams.
Rivers slowed down, and marshes grew.
Fish and small mammals flourished.

Custer

Custer wore an arrow shirt, or so they say.
What obsession filled his mind that fateful day?
Was it his duty, or did he believe the lies,
manifest destiny his singular objective?

We see the snag that briefly stopped
the march of time. We call that event
Custer's last stand - a fleeting victory
for those who opposed him.

President Grant sent his old friend
William Tecumseh Sherman
To exterminate the buffalo. He said,
"Every dead buffalo is an Indian gone."

The mission schools restricted worship to Sundays.
They stripped away their native ways and language,
and forbade the children to wear native clothing.
They did their best to obliterate a culture.

A web of deceit entangled them and
took them to apartheid reservations, but
the Sun Dance continues around the Cottonwood,
and the medicine wheel remains unbroken.

The traditions are reborn every time
An indigenous person wields the power of NO.

Impressionist Paintings

When I take off my glasses
the world becomes
an impressionist painting.

Infused with light
the purple flowers
shimmer and vibrate.

Impressionist brush strokes
visible with juxtaposed colors
record the passage of time.
They give birth to fauvism and cubism.

Dali's clock melts and the canvas yields
a completed painting,
as Gauguin sets sail for Tahiti
and Picasso fractures physical planes.

Money

When it comes to money there is never enough.
People with plenty say times are tough.

For those without, times are tougher still.
There's no cash in the house to pay that bill.

Adam Smith said we will always want more
to buy new goods; keep the wolf from the door.

The wolf is what we always perceive.
Your wealth is determined by what you believe.

I examine my bills and check my account,
as I wish I had a larger amount.

Reincarnation

An old black vulture landed in a tree
overlooking Chickamauga Creek
and gave me a sidelong glance.

I thought of Edward Abbey,
the critic of government agencies,
professor and park ranger.

Abbey is buried in an illegal grave.
A cairn of stones covers his remains.

His friends saw to his request,
wrote on one stone,
"Edward Abbey, no comment."

The nemesis of Glen Canyon Dam
desired no memorial but got one anyway.

He always said he'd come back
as a vulture next time.
It just seemed fitting.

I looked up into the oak, and said,
"Hey there Ed,
it looks like a good day for flying."

Abbey didn't say a word.
He just gave me that sidelong glance,
the old buzzard.

It Begins

Some-one coaxes you to serve on a committee,
fill a term on a board of directors,
become an officer or take this job.

You spend your hope and enthusiasm on the project
like a nebula pouring matter into a black hole.

The chain tightens, binds you to your idea
as it becomes a separate universe
with a gravitational pull so strong you can't leave.

Like B.B. King, you start to sing,
"The Thrill is Gone."
Your colleagues look at you strangely,
wondering why they brought you on board.

But you keep working like a piston in an engine,
as your quest to reach the transformative moment
seems a will-o-the-wisp, a desert mirage.

You see your colleagues resist change until
the organization is a putrid scent in your nostrils.

You would trade your treasure for a vacation
or a float trip on a river, but you settle for
a walk in the park and a few roadside blackberries.

You give up, walk away, and count yourself lucky
to get out so cheaply. When a friend casually
mentions the project, you want to scream.

Salvador Dali Meets Gertrude Stein

Nebulous nebulae, nebulae, nebulae nebulous
Navigate nebulous nebulae,
Oversee the weather, cloudy and serene.
Serene sirens negotiate nebulous nebulae
with squad cars of the intergalactic police
as we negotiate a tapestry
of weather symbols and barrel staves
in water inhabited by golden goldfish and
copper piranhas. Copper cop car piranhas
eat us out of house and home,
house and home house, house, home.

Ascend cirrus cloud, cloud, cloud, cirrus stairs.
Find no piranhas here but chum for sharks.
Catch any sharks, chum? Chum, chum, chum
for tiger, tiger, burning bright, tiger sharks
pursue us on this journey with no destination
to love but the question itself of who
ate the last shark steak in the refrigerator.
Shark steak, steak, steak, shark steak shark.

Man-eating shark has a stake in this tale and
has a tail to tell it with like Ferlinghetti's dog,
if indeed it is the shark that eats the man and.
not the man eating the shark stake,
the SOB took the last one.
Gnash your teeth you sharkless humans
and humorless sharks. Gnash, gnash, teeth, teeth
gnash human teeth gnash on shark flesh irony.

Slime Mold

A pulsing blob of gelatin wriggled across my path.
Amoeba-like it crept along the forest floor.
Scoop it into a glass. Pour it out like water.

Plant or animal - resolve the enigma of its existence.
It slipped into a wormhole and emerged
at the base of a tree to climb upward.

I slipped into a wormhole and crossed the galaxy.
Let others puzzle out the mystery of my voyage.
I grin remembering the journey.

Time Travel

Time Travelers
are out of time
in fractured space.

We avoid collapsing stars
and traverse an expanding universe.

The universe breathes in
and space expands.
Distant light shifts to red.

The universe breathes out
and space contracts.
Distant light shifts blue.

Does the universe become purple
in a moment of stasis
as expansion ends and contraction begins?

My universe expands
each time I open a book.
It contracts as I clean the house.

Ocoee Dam Deli and Diner

It's conveniently located near a dam.
The name provides infinite marketing opportunities.
"Dam Staff" is emblazoned on servers' shirts,
the word liberally sprinkled throughout the menu.

I chose the Garden Dam Wrap, nestled among
Dam Burgers, Dam Salads, and other dam selections.
A veggie burger wrapped in a soft shell,
it's topped with salsa, lettuce, and cheese.

I found the black bean soup worth the upcharge,
substituted for the normal fries or chips.
It was a real meal after three turkey sandwich lunches,
my regular fare for days on the road.

Informal attire rules the day, t-shirts and shorts,
No bathing suits allowed. The rule endorses
proper attire and health department regulations.

Crowded with adventurous souls
ready for a whitewater trip,
or just finished with one,
the place looks prosperous.

I wonder how they will do in January.
No matter how they do, it's dam good food.

Advice in Time of Plague

Do not Abandon all hope ye who enter here
nor let the weight of current events crush your soul.
Mourn what is lost, but not too long.
Crush the hurdle of despair and
the dark thoughts lurking there.
Pitch a tent near cool mountain streams.
Lay spoil to grim demeanor and resurrect hope.
Revel in the comedy of a fence lizard's display.
Delight in wild violets and trout lilies.
Never forget you are called to live.

Mike

With an internal rhyme scheme, he told of a dream
of California haze and his surfer days
perhaps spent in a daze after Vietnam.

I wondered about that shark tattoo outlined in blue.
Through the water, it flew as it sat on his arm
to protect him from harm. It failed in the end.

When Covid struck, he was out of luck,
no one passed the buck. The doctors tried,
but on a ventilator, he died in a hospital room.

They folded the flag and gave a salute with
twenty-one guns and a bugle to boot.
On Federal land, he made his last stand.

With hope, I say, "We'll meet again someday
in a land far away." We may toast him with cheer
if heaven allows beer and hear a few poems.

Family

One grandma died young.
At age 12, mama became her nurse.
She helped the lady of the house
to the porch so she could sew in the sun.
Her father called her "our little nurse."

Each morning, she packed her daddy's lunch,
an unasked question on her lips
the day he dropped a pistol into the lunch box.

The miners were on strike.
He walked the picket line
wary of company goons.
"Don't let anyone in the house.
Those company men are tricky."

He once said that a man
walked up to him in the mine,
conversed for a few minutes,
and faded into the wall.

Another grandma succumbed to madness
when her husband abandoned her
with all those kids.

The orphanage kindly welcomed Papa.
Two maiden aunts took him in
so he could go to high school.

Now I have gone and done it.
I have dropped my guard and wonder
how much I should let you see through my disguise.
Perhaps I will let in just a little light.

We may have been poor, but we owned land.
The garden fed us all summer.
Mason jars of beans, tomatoes, and corn
fed us most of the winter,
supplemented with rabbit and pheasant
from the old man's game pouch.

Trips to the store were occasional
for grits, coffee, sugar, and bacon.
Mama's hens provided eggs until
the zoning commission said they had to go.

Some nights, I slept in my tent.
Daytime, I read in its shade,
my companion a hound dog,
barely grown from a pup.
I named her Babe after
Paul Bunyan's blue ox.

I read every story I could
about that legend of a man.
His frying pan was so big
two lumberjacks skated across its surface
with slabs of bacon strapped to their feet.

When the blue ox Babe stopped for a drink,
the Round River ran dry.

Before I left fundamentalism behind,
they dunked me in the water:
Three times!
Once for the father!
Once for the son!
Once for the Holy Ghost!
I emerged primarily unchanged.

Repurposed Clothing

The naked trees have no shame.
Without blame, they shed their leaves.
As nature weaves a cloak of color.

Leaves depart to cover the ground
where they are found on the forest floor.
What is more, they shelter wildflowers.

Safe and warm in leafy blankets
The flowers snuggle in winter form,
until reborn to dance in golden sunlight.

Spider Eyes

What does a spider see with her eight eyes?
Descending to an anchor point to fix
her silken thread upon the hardened bricks.

I see a roof caved in beside that ruin
where the paint had peeled away like empty dreams.
What does a spider see with her eight eyes?

A tree springs up, new life among the boards,
no comfort to a family now gone
descending to an anchor point to fix

their broken lives as Spider spins her web.
She sees crickets do their Danse Macabre within
her silken thread upon the hardened bricks.

Nature's Decorum

Deep in the woods, I let go of proper decorum.
Distant neighbors will not hear me howl.
As the moon sends forth her magic beams,
Diana drives her chariot across the sky.

No one will see me dance with wild abandon
as morning star Venus sends forth her light
or evening star Venus greets the crescent moon.
Deep in the woods, I let go of proper decorum.

Coyotes celebrate the moon and become song dogs.
Domestic dogs may join with yaps of memory,
as silent Sirius faithfully follows Orion skyward.
Distant neighbors will not hear me howl.

Fancy seizes me on active sleepless nights.
I sit on my porch to watch the dipper rise
and seek the bear in stars made faint by city lights.
As the moon sends forth her magic beams.

I imagine druids dancing beneath the oaks
as friends gather at a fire with drums and chants.
Sun and moon strike stones of distant lands
and Diana drives her chariot across the sky.

Walking the Labyrinth
October 2013

The path of the soul is not linear.
It spirals like the turns of this maze,
outlined with bricks on their sides.
Like time, it circles back
passes by starting points.

I turn left, one hundred eighty degrees.
Not exactly the way I came, this path
to the center, where there is no Minotaur.
My dragons are all in my heart,
slain or otherwise.

The first wall outlines a square
which no paths cross.
Is this square sacred ground,
reserved for shaman, priestess,
and holy man?

If I stepped inside where
no tracks appear, would I
transport to another place or time,
reappear burned to ash
by sacred Geometry?

A friend asked a transit driver
in Nashville's less sacred geometry,
Is this my stop? Her simple reply,
"Either sit back down or get off the bus."

Dream of the River

Dreaming of you I took the mountain road.
In my old red pickup truck, I drove
through mountain passes, saw the river below,
with its rapids white as the glint of ice.

Crossing the streambed, I found the water too high.
Too late to turn back I washed downstream.
I passed kayaks and white-water rafts.
The river was lapping just below my windows.

Kayakers shook their fists, raft guides struggled,
and customers screamed as I careened into their paths.
I climbed through the window onto the open bed.
Ropes thrown from shore dropped short of me.

The truck crashed into a boulder
at a bend in the river. Thrown to the current,
I scrambled to the bank. There I stood,
shivering in new-fallen snow

For the Last Carolina Parakeet

I imagine the loneliness of your aviary
there at the Cincinnati Zoo where your
predecessor, the last Passenger Pigeon
flew off to oblivion just a few years earlier.
One voice is not a choir.

You were part of a social species,
descending by the thousands,
on fields to consume cockleburs,
or orchards for luscious fruits.
One voice is not a choir.

Some labeled you a pest
and pursued you with shotguns.
Audubon noticed your species
in decline even in his bygone days.
One voice is not a choir.

No welcoming song of your fellows
greeted your waning days. Does your
skin adorn a museum, just as your
ancestors' feathers adorned lady's hats?
One voice is not a choir.

It saddens me to think my adopted home
of Tennessee once knew the calls and colors
of a native parrot. One scientist titled
an article about your demise, "Forever Gone."
No voices remain in the choir.

The Songs of Rivers

They are stilled by dams, though
bass notes still resound in depths,
and lull catfish to sleep.

The tremolo of rapids is lost
to navigational safety.
Lament is the silenced symphony.

The river waves to fishermen on shore.
"Heed the sign, keep away from the outflow,
unless you wish to kiss the muddy depths."

Below the dam, the river accelerates,
sings of crickets and raindrops from its youth,
up there, at its mountain birthplace.

It's Just a Phase

The full moons are the extrovert's moons.
They are dedicated to performance poetry.
The new moons are the introvert's moons.
They are dedicated to memoirs and essays.
The First Quarter moons are the fiction writer's moons.
The Last Quarter moons are the nonfiction writer's moons.
The waxing moons are the poet's moons.
The waning moons are the publisher's moons.
Crescent moons are the niche market moons,
the brightest spot in a writer's life.
Eclipsed moons are the empath's moons,
Reminding writers to have empathy for their characters.

Renaming the Full Moons

One Christmas day I saw the ducks
dancing in a courtship ritual.
December is the Dancing Duck Moon.

One year, Glen Falls became a booming choir.
January is the Moon of Rain and Flood.

On a mountain road lonely enough
to break your heart
I saw a family of foxes.
I declare February the Fox Kit Moon.

The warming earth makes March
the Singing Frog Moon.
It is also the Bloodroot Moon.

Azaleas and Dogwoods bloom in April.
The Ospreys zoom over rivers and lakes,
but April is the Trillium Moon.

Still learning to hunt,
young hawks resort to roadkill.
They return to the nest to find mom gone.
May is the Young Hawks Hunting Moon.

June is the Scorpio Moon.
The scorpion shines brightly in the southern sky.
It is a time for bonfires and music.

July is the Sunflower Moon.
It is also the Moon When I Saw a Rattlesnake.
She glided in circles beside the road.

August is the Spiderling Moon.
It is a collage of nature's colors and sounds.

September is the Katydid Moon.
I hear them singing in the night.
Who was Katy, and what did she do?

October is the Moon when Maple Leaves Turn Red.
It is also the Pumpkin Moon.

November is the Bare Branches Moon.
I see the river when leaves are off the trees.

The year is complete, and it is December again.
Early December is the Time When Cranes Return.
Hoping to see these old friends, I scan the sky.

Old Moon

Ask the moon, she knows
what transpires under oaks.
Old Moon, Mother Earth's sister,
blesses orchids as they grow.

A coyote howls at the moon. Ocean waves
reflect her light and respond to her pull.
My heart longs for the distant sea,
With moon and stars reflected in her pools.

Tiny diatoms give luminescent tide,
each one a spark on moonless nights.
With Orion, I pursue the seven sisters
and wait for the moon to bless the seasons.

Seals rest as dolphins leap.
A full moon at daybreak greets Cape Cod Bay.
Long-tailed ducks, harlequin, and scooter
dive for fish under the cold moon.

A warm moon appears, and I see Jellyfish
among the mangroves. Key West Beckons.

Old Stone Fort

The paved entrance to a stone enclosure
aligns with the sun on the summer solstice.

Excavations revealed carved shell gorgets
and ornate breastplates which
complement skull bone rattles.

Are those skulls honored ancestors?
Are they a human sacrifice?

Dance to greet the sun within ancient walls.
Venerate the long day. Anticipate the harvest.

Under a setting sun, barrows fill in.
Walls wear low as stones fall to the valley below.

New ceremonies grace a waning moon.
The moon went behind the clouds, millennia ago,
and dancers worked magic moments in scared time.

Moonbow

Have you seen the moonbow?
I don't mean the rainbow,
light fractured by raindrops.

Pale moonbeams pierce mist
thrown upward by a waterfall,
each appearance a month apart.

To see the moonbow, you must go,
to the Cumberland Mountain
not the plateau,

where fiddlers exchange a tune,
and water tumbles through the mist
in a halo of light and sound.

Coyote Land

Go down to the raging waterfall.
Where even the full moon cannot pierce
the darkness that gathers under pines.

Sit beside the fire as embers die.
Sleep despite the noise of owls,
their cackling calls like monkeys.

That's when coyotes come,
ears alert to any threat.
Soft feet make no sound.

Fathered by a wild dog,
grandson of a she-wolf,
he's not like Western kin,

Far from desert lands
silent forest creature stalks
within a foot of fires and tents.

He wakes you with manic laughter
of souls condemned to echo
in the calls of loons.

The Animals Hold a Congress

One day, the animals held a congress.
They came from all around and met
on the banks of a mountain stream
so that Trout and his kin could attend.

They held it in winter before
the birthing season so mothers
could attend without young to tend.
Everyone wanted to be included.

Bear agreed to be the moderator.
She was sleepy and knew that
a new cub was on the way soon,
but the others trusted her wisdom.

Deer and Big-horned Sheep were nervous
at seeing wolf and cougar attending,
but ancient agreements had been invoked,
no hunting would take place that day.

Everyone was there except the Humans.
The barred owl had traveled far
to deliver the invitation, but the Humans
had forgotten the meaning of their songs.

The Hellbender

Hellbender – North America's largest Salamander.
They dine on fish, crayfish, and aquatic insects.

She curls among the tumbled rocks
and waits for a crayfish dinner.
If she doesn't find a crawdad soon,
tomorrow she will be thinner.

She will happily eat a frog or fish,
for she's an agile swimmer.
But the crawdad is a favorite dish,
it causes her eye to glimmer.

Beneath the rocks, she laid her eggs.
There must have been a hundred or more.
At parenting, she is the dregs.
She ate a few just to even the score.

Her mate saw this act and chased her away
If eating eggs, she just couldn't stay.
He guarded those eggs till they hatched one day.
Then he swam away much slimmer.

Editor's Note

Welcome to our green issue.
In these pages, you will find
we care about the environment,
so we went white water rafting.

You, too, can travel down
Tennessee's Ocoee River
where rocks have been moved
to sculpt a natural waterway
suitable for Olympic competitions.

This issue's featured artists
exhibit their love of nature by
making ornate wooden bowls
from carefully selected trees.

Our dining section features
an Irish pub. What could be
more appropriate for
the wearing of the green?

Our message this month is
"Green Goes Mainstream."
Sorry to say it's printed
on glossy, non-recycled paper.

As one of our advertisers says,
at their import emporium,
you can buy locally
while shopping globally

Homeward

A dark shadow beneath the clouds
swoops faster than the wind.

Talons sharp as knives
snatch a squirrel.

A Red-tailed Hawk flies homeward.

All too soon,
feathers, flesh, and sinew
return to dust.

Only bones remain.

Miami by Greyhound

I was in at three am, waiting for
a seven o'clock out to Key West.

The dirty dogs came and went all night.
A man warned me not to fall asleep.

I realized his wisdom as a Danish tourist
got his passport stolen.

Then I was on the road, dreaming of
Alligator Alley; imagining Everglades.

I ate a hamburger at Islamorada,
and saw palm trees through the window.

The engine hummed in my dreams as
saltwater flowed beneath the bridges.

The rattling floor of the Greyhound bus
shook beneath my feet.

Key West, 1980

The horizon was not salmon,
to match the belly of the fish,
nor was it red as the belly of a rainbow trout.

It turned pink as the inside
of a polished conch shell
I nearly bought on the docks there.

The sky turned violet
as the ink of a sea hare,
a marine slug I once
picked up in shallow waters.

In those days the sun set directly into the ocean.
Revelers lined the docks to drum and dance.

Acrobats, jugglers, fire eaters,
and parrots on silver chains,
watched the sunset.

We drifted off to Sloppy Joes
to dance beneath the gaze of Papa,
Hemingway painted on a wall.
A patron blessing his flock?

Recipe for Love

Take two marginally sane people.
Place in an extra-large mixing cup.
Add vodka, sugar, and lemon juice.
Set vodka on fire.
Add ice! Quickly!

Serve shaken.

Time's Geography

Behind the waterfall,
the reds and blues sparkle and shine.

Behind the rushing stream,
the illusions form and dissolve.

Leaving the falls
the droplets flow downstream.

I emerge from the river, from underwater currents.
Water flows down my chest and arms.

A fire of driftwood warms me.
Logs burned cannot grow again.

I cannot cross time's geography to when
I held you close and felt the beat of your heart.

I collect my belongings from your carport,
leave my key, and float downstream.

Publication Credits

Villanelle for the Didgeridoo appeared in *Tennessee Voices*, the 2022-2023 Poetry Society of Tennessee Anthology.

Salvadore Dali Meets Gertrude Stein appeared in *2nd and Church*, Nashville.

Reincarnation appeared in *Southern Light: Twelve Contemporary Southern Poets*.

The Hellbender appeared in *Tennessee Magazine*.

Impressionist Paintings appeared in Quill and Parchment and was republished in The Weekly Avocet.

Late August Collage and Driving to New Hope appeared in *Catalpa*.

Advice in Time of Plague, Mike, and Family appeared in the *Mildred Haun Review*.

For the Last Carolina Parakeet appeared in *Number One*, Gallatin, Tennessee.

Published in *The Avocet* or *The Weekly Avocet:*
The Songs of Rivers
Repurposed Clothing
Nature's Decorum

Published in my out-of-print DIY chapbook, *Searching for Cranes*:
Editor's Note
Homeward
Old Moon
Old Stone Fort

Moonbow
Recipe For Love
Miami by Greyhound
Key West, 1980
Time's Geography
Dream of the River

Author Biography

Ray Zimerman is a former president of the Chattanooga Writers Guild and the Chattanooga Audubon Society. He enjoys photographing, drawing, and writing about the natural world.

Ray's poetry and prose have appeared in several publications. He leads nature writing workshops at The Chattery, an educational organization in Chattanooga, and various other venues.

If you wish to comment on these works, please use the contact form on Ray Zimmerman's website, https://rayzimmermanauthor.com. More of Ray's work is available on the Substack page: https://rayzimmerman.substack.com.

www.ingramcontent.com/pod-product-compliance
Lightning Source LLC
Chambersburg PA
CBHW011240120626
46549CB00009B/3352